11 Steps To Tech
>_Zack_Amin

```
const inspire = ("Hello Work")
console.log(inspire)
```

What The Bootcamp Doesn't Teach You
v1.0

Copyright © Zack Amin 2021

All rights reserved. No portion of the book may be reproduced or utilized in any form or by any means, electronic or mechanical, including photocopying, recording, or by any other information storage and retrieval system, without permission in writing from the author.

Prologue

After a recent event I hosted circa, lockdown number 'Math.floor(Math.random() *100)' (giggles in JavaScript), I put together a thank you email.

This event was aimed at junior developers looking to grow in their careers or aspiring developers looking to enter the industry.

There were two fantastic speakers; <u>Fey Ijaware</u> and <u>Zack Akil</u>. Who talked about some interesting topics, which I came to realise were all the steps I had taken to land my first and second role as a junior software engineer.

The thank you email, I just mentioned, covered eleven points every aspiring and junior developer should follow to land that elusive first role in tech.

Some points were technical, whilst some points were personal. They all laid the foundation of what companies and hiring managers look for in potential candidates and what you can do to stand out from the rest.

I know following these eleven points will work.

As following them is how I got my my first role and am more successful in my second.

After being an electrician for ten-years I transitioned into tech. It was hard, really hard. However, it has paid off in ways I couldn't have imagined back then.

Being quite active on social media and as a mentor, I have had the pleasure of working with and meeting various people from tech leads to scrum masters, from Google engineers to government. Having the opportunity to ask questions and figure out what those new to the industry are missing, from my own experience and others.

On a final note, this book is meant to be a guide for people who are aiming to land their first role as a junior software engineer.

It will show you how to build a solid foundation and explain what you need to do and know to stand out from the crowd.

The unique difference people who are self-taught or bootcamp graduates often miss out is that you need to build a documented history of your learning through projects.

Essentially, it is proving that you can do what your CV claims you can.

Some parts may not directly impact you, for example, if you are a university graduate you may already have projects to show potential employers. If that is the case then this book will guide you in other areas, social media and tech tests, etc.

This book will cover the eleven points in detail, along with some personal perspective, a swear word or two and even some humour from myself, a some what successful self-taught software engineer with ambitions to see other people succeed.

Let's dive in.

Table of Contents

1. Do you have a Github? No. Erm, Ok....................7

2. Half a project is better than no project. 13

3. CV, Yes please!..18

4. Passion projects > tutorial projects.....................26

5. Just apply, learn it when you get the job. 33

6. Be brave little one..39

7. Show me the money...51

8. Social media…ah shit..57

9. We have anxiety too!..66

10. Code makes us all cry. 71

11. Failure happens, success is imminent................80

Common interview questions / tech test skills for junior positions..84

1. Do you have a Github? No. Erm, Ok.

> *Having a GitHub account is a big yes! It allows people to not only see how much you have done, but also what. Fey, one of our fantastic speakers said, "I am not too interested in how often you upload, but what you have uploaded."*

Ah, Github.

You beautiful thing.

First we will cover GitHub then the Git itself.

For those of you who may have no idea who a GitHub is. Well, for starters, it is a what.

GitHub is probably one of the most used pieces of software in the industry. It is a platform for hosting code and collaboration between teams.

They have close to 60 million users and it is free for developers like you and me.

You can connect your GitHub account to the projects you create and push the code to your GitHub repository for others to see as well as pull other people's code down.

There are awesome things like branching, merge requests, a dashboard which shows how often you upload projects and more.

You are probably now wondering, 'that sounds great, what does it have to do with me?'

Well to answer the question, I am hoping you just asked, this is what is has to do with you.

Your GitHub account is just as, if not more, valuable than your CV.

Let that sink in for just a second.

You and I have always been taught the importance of an up to date CV.

It has to be this or that long, contain some or no references, maybe a little about you but not too much about you, a little colour is Ok, nope that's too much colour… you get the point.

Your GitHub is your opportunity to show companies and recruiters what you are capable of and showcase your hunger to learn.

It takes what you claim to be able to do and proves it.

If you have written a little if/else script in javascript? Push it to your GitHub.

Maybe you made a little game in Python? Push it to your GitHub.

Got a half finished website in React? Push it to your GitHub.

I should imagine you're getting the picture about now.

You maybe thinking back to the start of this chapter, when I mentioned what Fey, said about quality of uploads over quantity, we will cover that in the next chapter.

As you are learning or coding, once your repo is connected to your project, pushing your code to GitHub takes around ten seconds.

Here is a picture of my GitHub dashboard from the last year.

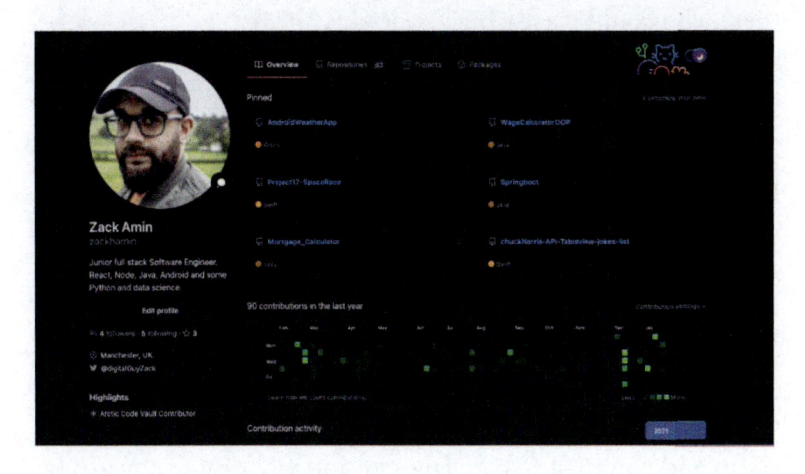

Obviously I use dark mode, because tech.

I also use incomplete sentences, because tech.

The little green squares represent the days and how often I made commits(pushed code to a repository). It shows 90 contributions(commits) over the last year.

Towards the top you can see a tab which says 'repositories 83', this is the total number of projects I have created.

Some terrible, some not so terrible. I have some projects pinned to the front. I change those around every now and then.

When a recruiter or a company shortlists you for a job they will look at your GitHub.

Your repos, your green squares and what tech you have been using plus what sort of projects you have been building.

Now GitHub is one of many code collaboration websites out there, you could use BitBucket or GitLab etc.

GitHub is just one of the more popular. All this may seem a little confusing right now, it will however be one of the most used tools in your career.

The second part to GitHub is the Git itself.

Not the hub.

Git is an open source version control software. Git allows people, teams and companies to collaborate and work more effectively.

Multiple people can work on the same project by branching, pushing, merging and more.

These terms will become more and more familiar to you as you get into your career.

Just imagine.

You are working for a company. You get a ticket which means making a change to the ui.

It's GIT time.

Create a new branch off of master in Github. Clone the repository to your desktop.

Open your favourite IDE. Checkout the branch. Write your code. Commit your changes. Push your changes to your branch. Create a merge request to be checked by your senior and then merged into master.

All while many other engineers are working on different parts of the same piece of software.

That is the power of understanding GIT, yet there is so much more to it.

For now just know, having a GitHub account and the ability to pull, push, commit and do basic version control commands will help you in landing your first role.

As you can now see, having a GitHub account is number one on the list for a a very good reason.

TAKE AWAY

If you have a GitHub account, use it.

Keep it neat.

If you do not have one, get one and learn how to use it.

A Github account will allow recruiters and companies to see your work. What sort of projects you have worked on and that you understand the basics of version control.

There is also much more to know about using GitHub. There are thousands of open source software projects on there for you to get involved in plus repos dedicated to code snippets, etc.

Considering you will likely spend the rest of your career using GIT and some form of hosting software Github, Gitlab, Bitbucket etc it is a good idea to have some experience with it!

2. Half a project is better than no project.

> **Do not be afraid of what you upload. Even if it isn't complete, explaining in the ReadMe or even in the code with a /*TODO: Comment*/ what you have left to do and how you plan to do it.**

As someone wanting to join the technology sector, there can be a lot of different feelings looking from the 'outside in'.

'Are my projects good enough?'

'No one wants to see a one page website'

'It's not finished I'd better not show it to anyone'.

When I first started pushing to GitHub, all of the above went through my mind. I had a mixture of feelings about more than just GitHub and projects.

However, I decided that I needed my GitHub showing work and I knew that any small amount of code would be better than no code.

Hence, half a project is better than no project.

Don't take this the wrong way. It isn't an invitation to start a new project every third day.

Something which I was very terrible for.

I mean who doesn't want to build a weather app, get half way through and start building space invaders? ahem.

You should try and stick to one tutorial or project until it is finished. Don't fall for the shiny spoon syndrome.

The point being, start pushing your project from the very first commit. If you think the project may take a while to complete, or you want to come back to it in the future there are things you can do to make it look more professional.

//TODO: comments

```
56
57
58      // TODO: add a function which takes an argument and returns a string
59
60
61
```

Throughout your professional career you will come across TODO comments in code, most often ones which you have left for yourself.

TODO comments are just a way of leaving little hints for what you need or plan to do.

DO NOT litter them everywhere, you do not need one on every other line. A simple comment with what you need or plan to do is enough.

This will show anyone who looks at your projects that you are capable of commenting code for the benefit of others and yourself, whilst also covering up the fact that you may not have returned to that particular project for five weeks.

The other option available to you is the README. When you create a new repository or project on GitHub you will get the option to generate a README file, or you can add your own.

In the README you can write a little about your project, what it does or plans to do and how far you have got, plus what you have left to do.

You could even do it as a checklist:

- Create header for web page
- Create body
- Add footer
- Call API
- Use JSON Stringify to deserialise JSON

Again, it is showing recruiters and companies that you are conscious about clear communication and collaboration.

You know your way around GitHub and you can plan your work.

TAKE AWAY

Push all your work to your GitHub.

It may seem a little counter intuitive, however when you are getting started it is a good habit to get into.

Do not leave empty repositories. Delete them, they look messy and are pointless.

Use comments and README files to write a little about your project and what the idea or plan is. When the project is complete write about what the project does and how to run it, start it and use it.

You can change around the projects which you have pinned to the front of your GitHub. If you are applying for a job in Javascript, pin some Javascript projects, etc.

What you are aiming for is to have a documented history of projects utilising the language of your choice. This documented history of learning and projects is what will allow you to stand out much more in applications!

It shows your ability to contribute to code, your skills with Git Version Control, collaboration and more.

3. CV, Yes please!

> *Your CV is your first step through the door. As developers there is plenty of advice out there on setting up your socials or your portfolio. What often gets overlooked is your CV.*

Socials? All optimised.

Portfolio? Done, built and hosted.

CV? Erm.

In my latest role, I got the opportunity to review candidates for Junior and some Mid level roles.

Prior to that, I also reviewed and helped to improve on many CVs which people in my network send to me when looking to land their first role into tech, or after being in their first role and were looking to their second.

I quickly began to pickup on small things which we, as creative people, tend to do which are not necessarily the best way to stand out.

This section is not meant to be expansive, CVs are a whole topic I, and many others, could write whole books up on. So, I will cover the basics in hopes that it helps you pass the first stage.

1. Please, triple check for spelling mistakes!

Yes, you would be surprised.

I have found minor spelling mistakes in even the most academic of CVs. This isn't a deal breaker, however having a friend or relative review your CV takes minutes.

There is no room for error at this stage, we want you so polished all the recruiter see's in your CV is their own reflection with money in their eyes!

2. Relax with the brackets and colour

Guilty as charged your honour.

I made a nice fancy CV, great layout with plenty of {text in brackets} I mean, I am applying to a tech job right?

Yeah, they aren't great.

Quite often the layout and information looks pretty, but it is not very practical to read. I redid a CV from someone looking to land their first role.

I removed all the fancy text, brackets and made it plain and simple. Within a week he had two interviews.

Coincidence?
I think not.

He had all the necessary skills and had a great portfolio, however his CV was hard to read and the layout was messy.

All CVs should be straight to the point, they are quickly skimmed and if the information the recruiters are after is obscured or not in an easy to digest layout, to the bin it goes.

3. Double check your links

When reviewing CVs I tend to always go through to the links and check out the projects the applicant is working on.

To my dismay and surprise, many of the links were broken.

It seemed very odd that someone would send a CV with links which were broken.

For such a small simple fix, it seems lazy. Either remove the links or fix them!

Please double check the links in your CV are actually working before sending it.

4. PDF or word format, please

Quite often CVs are read by people with different machines. If you use a Mac and save your word document as a .pages it may not open for the person reading it.

Navigate this issue in a super simple way. Either save it as a PDF and send the PDF or save it as a word document(docx) on Mac which means whoever receives it can read it.

5. Take out non-relevant information

Remove fluff. Anything which isn't related to the job or career that you want.

Previous jobs can be included if they are relevant based on experience or if you learned transferable skills from them.

If not then include them together in one or two paragraphs explaining what you were doing in them prior to being on your new career path.

6. Utilise what you achieved

One of the hardest things to get right on a CV is essentially, bragging about yourself. I get it, humble by nature.

Writing your CV, however, is one of those very few times in life where you will get massively rewarded for being your own biggest fan.

Using numbers, descriptive words etc can show that you are not just a follower, but a do-er.

If you increased annual turn over, tell them how much by.

If you made an impact on customer satisfaction, what was the impact on the company?

You can also list your bootcamp or self-taught experience as your latest job.

Many people undersell what they learned and did on their bootcamps.

For example..

Bootcamp - Junior Developer
(January 2021 – March 2021)

- Learned how to code using Javascript, React and Node.
- Attended daily stand-ups and utilised Agile ways of working.
- Collaborated with team members to build projects using GitHub and Git version control.
- Acted as product owner for project using Kanban boards and sprint planning.
- Built UI's following best practices and React library utilising hooks, state and props.

etc.

Get descriptive. Those keywords are there to be picked up. Show that you are capable of working in a team and that you are eager to continue on.

7. Only put down tech you can talk about

This should be number one. More often than not I get approached to look at a CV and they have a huge shopping list of tech, python, JS, React, Node, Mongo, Typesript, SQL, NOSQL etc, etc.

So, I ask a question.

Tell me what interfaces are used for in Typescript? Tell me how OOP (object orientated programming) works in Python?

Guess what?

They stutter and have no idea.

Now, I do not do this to make people upset, I do it to prepare them. Whatever you have on your CV is open season when it comes to interviews.

If you have a load of tech, which you used for a week in your bootcamp, and you cannot answer basic questions about it - It is going to look bad.

If you have a relatively small number of things you have used, which you are comfortable answering questions on then you will look much more confident and stand out.

TAKE AWAY

CVs are like opinions, everyone has one and no two are often alike. The best thing you can do at this point in your career is KISS.

Keep It Simple Stupid.
- ❖ Stick to relevant information.
- ❖ Leave the fancy designs for graphic designers.
- ❖ Have your information clear and concise.
- ❖ Utilise numbers to show impact.
- ❖ Use descriptive words.
- ❖ Be your own biggest fan.
- ❖ Have live links to your socials and projects.
- ❖ Only put down things you can talk about.

Please, always get someone to double check for spelling errors and broken links.

Do not list every piece of tech you have ever worked with, unless you are prepared to talk about it.

Doing Python for a week on your bootcamp is great, but it can also be a danger point as it gives the interviewer another thing to ask you about.

The final takeaway is to make sure your CV is relevant to the jobs your are applying for. If you are applying for a Python job but all your projects and learning has been Javascript, what does this say?

Tailor your CV to the role you want.

4. Passion projects > tutorial projects.

> *If you are presenting a project, something which you are passionate about will come across a lot more in an interview than something which you are not. As Zack Akil said, "a personal project, even if it has no real-world application can still be exciting".*

Oh, so you have made a '*insert social media site*' clone? Nice. Have a seat over there with the 14,000 others.

If you attend a bootcamp or follow a tutorial you are likely to have made one of the below;

- Twitter clone
- Instagram clone

- ❖ Netflix clone
- ❖ Note taking app
- ❖ Weather app
- ❖ Calculator
- ❖ Other generic project

During tech interviews, recruiters are very interested in what you have made, created or built.

It is the name of the game, after all.

However, the ability to become overly generic in what you do at the beginning of your career is a curse.

Just imagine for a moment you followed some tutorials / attended your bootcamp.

Great.

You get an interview and your interviewer asks, 'so I saw this Netflix clone, made from React, in your GitHub…Tell me about it?', knowing full well he has seen ten before it.

'Erm yeah, it is made in React. It uses props which passes data and reusable components plus it uses functional components instead of class.'

Boring.

9 times out of 10 you will not realise but speaking about something you are not passionate about resonates in your tone.

Now, following the tutorial itself, is not a bad thing.

We all have to learn.

Here are **two ways** to spin this in your favour.

1. Get out of your comfort zone

This is something I share time and time again at events and to people I advise and mentor.

If you are following a tutorial, and you're comfortable enough to do so, try and change it up a little.

You may start with something small, like the tutorial uses a red button, so you find the code to use a blue button.

Maybe they show you how to call a weather API so you then take that code, import it to another project, change the URL and pull data from a different API..Maybe the Star Wars API?

Tutorials will teach you some skill, yet it is so easy to get stuck in tutorial purgatory.

When you start thinking outside the box and making small changes you will really start to grow and learn as a developer.

It will force you into a position where you have to think why something doesn't work, maybe you need to search Stack Overflow or ask a question?

It pushes you out of your comfort zone and gives you another project to talk about.

Surely, a better response would be…

'So, I made a Netflix clone and that was great, however, what I really love is that I managed to take what I learned there and make *this* app in React which does *so and so*.

I struggled implementing *this* but I managed to find an example on Stack Overflow and got it working in the end.'

Straight away you are more excited. It comes across in your body language, your tone and your face. I mean how long has it been since you smiled because you're excited about something you built?.

Why shouldn't you? You freakin built something cool AF. Be proud of it.

2. Personal projects over tutorials

Personal projects show way more enthusiasm and desire than followed tutorials or bootcamp projects.

When you have an idea, thought about it, built it, it fails so you research, find faults, build some more, it shows in your work.

As mentioned above, the energy and effort you put in will really show.

I will share a personal story with you about how this helped me land my first role…

I had an interview with a bank, prior to this I had been teaching myself mobile development, Swift to be precise.

I had an idea to create an app. This app was just a small little project to get me thinking and learning more.

The idea was, when you're out (or in), with a group of friends you often cannot decide on what to eat.

So, you open my app, give your phone a shake and it pops a little image giving you a choice of food, that could be Thai, Indian, Fish and Chips etc.

I built the app, I then used Apple's TestFlight app to put it on my phone.

It was a real app now. I was amazed. Super excited. I mean I built an app and now it was on my phone.

In my interview I was going against a lot of juniors who all had a similar background. We had the same type of projects.

I had my secret weapon though.

When talking to the recruiters, who were both senior software engineers I couldn't wait to show them my app, even though the role was for a backend engineer.

I showed them, let them use it, we had a laugh and a giggle, the interview got a lot more relaxed and five minutes later I had the job offer.

I know for a fact that I was going against some fantastic people. What set me apart was my passion project.

On a final note, your projects should not end because you do get your first job.

Building things is what helps you hone your craft, try new techniques and improve on your overall knowledge.

Not only that, but what you learn on the job will help you to build more advanced projects. I experienced this myself with what I am currently building, a full-stack job site, using React, Node, AWS and more.

What I have learned on the job has made it much easier for me to tackle such a big project and to understand more about the architecture and set up of a full stack application.

TAKE AWAY

Tutorials are a fantastic tool when it comes to learning new things, however, do not become overly dependant on them.

When you learn something from a tutorial think about how you can use it somewhere else, maybe an API call with a new endpoint or a UI layout which you can use in another project with different information.

Think about something fun you would like to build. A problem you would like to solve or just the most wackiest idea you can think of.

A project made from passion will show much more enthusiasm and allow you to stand out from the crowd.

It does not need to have a real world use, it can be just for fun!

5. Just apply, learn it when you get the job.

> **Apply for every junior role. It does not matter if it asks for a year of experience. What companies are more interested in is are you willing to learn. As long as you have some basics, they will teach you the rest.**

'I can't apply for that. It says you need five years experience, but it is asking for a junior? What even is life?'

Ok. Maybe that was a little bit of an over-statement. Yet, I bet many of you feel the same way.

For many companies, taking on junior developers is a new thing. Yes, really.

Apprentices, interns and junior engineers are more popular now more than ever.

Especially self taught programmers.

This is both fantastic and a bit of a problem.

The problems are basic things like having over-reaching job descriptions asking for juniors with years of experience or having worked with multiple languages, etc.

You see, companies scare away fantastic self-taught programmers or fantastic self-taught programmers feel too scared to apply to a role when reading job descriptions.

In my journey I applied to every damn thing.

Maybe sometimes I got a little too over confident and applied to things I shouldn't

Like the time I applied for a SOC analyst role and couldn't answer any questions on network ports or what they do..doh.

I digress..

Most companies do not know what they want in a junior developer.

They copy and paste a generic template from another company, add in some fancy buzz words like React, MongoDB, Node, Git, AWS and hey presto, you have a horrible job advertisement.

This just screams 'we want to pay as little as possible but get the most work out of you as we can.'

Now, armed with this information, it can either scare you or inspire you.

I mean if they are not sure what they want, why would they want you?

Or…if they are not sure what they want, **why not you?**

If you opt for the latter then you will likely have success in landing your first role.

If you opt for the former you will struggle throughout your whole career.

This is an industry and career path which is forever evolving- a constant challenge of adapting and learning.

Which is why you should always apply.

You will find companies are willing to take chances on people who are open to learning and have the right enthusiasm / desire to learn.

For example I started my journey as a mobile developer, as you may recall from the last chapter.

My second role was full-stack. React, Node, AWS, with some Java and other bits sprinkled in.

I had barely any experience with any of those technologies.

Did that scare me or stop me?

no, it did not.

I hit the interview and told them I am willing to try and without doubt I will learn whatever I need to do to get the job done. I should add, though I did have a years worth of proven experience as a developer, which of course backed up my ability to learn.

Hence 'Just apply, learn it when you get the job.'

This should also be your mantra.

If you want to be a software developer or engineer you will no doubt in your career have to understand a new tech, get comfortable with a new language or learn a new library.

Be open and honest.

When applying let your enthusiasm for learning and being a part of the industry flow through.

A junior with the enthusiasm to learn is a bigger asset than a senior who refuses to adapt or change.

Now, I have told you what you want to hear, here is the part you need to hear. There will be rejections.

Many, many rejections. I had countless rejections from companies without even so much as giving me a second glance.

Take it in your stride. Every no is just one step closer to an offer. The hardest part about rejections is finding the strength to keep going.

I know, as I always say, the right company will give you a shot. You just need to keep going until you find that company.

TAKE AWAY

A lot of companies are new to taking on junior engineers. Apply to them all, be willing and enthusiastic to learn.

More often than not you will read quite daunting job descriptions which are asking for way more than you're capable of at the moment.

Do not let this scare you off. Throughout your career you will be required to try new things. It is part of the excitement of working in technology.

As you apply to more jobs, you will face rejections, this is part and parcel of finding a new career. Just know, it isn't just you and your next job is just around the corner.

Be patient, sooner or later the right company will give you an opportunity.

6. Be brave little one.

> *If you are attempting a tech-test for a company, do not be afraid to ask questions to clarify what it is asking you to do.*
>
> *Do not be afraid to ask people for help, most importantly if you cannot complete it...still send it! You can add notes about how you would've completed it if you could, how it could be scalable etc.*

Tech tests, the stuff of nightmares for any career changer or self-taught programmer.

Are they really the be all and end all to your application?

Those who know me, will know my stance.

I believe most tech tests are horrendous.

I will share with you why.

A lot of companies send the same tech test to junior and senior developers.

They may not expect the same level of work being sent back, yet the initial concept is the same.

There are companies who write their own tech tests, which maybe along the lines of...

- ❖ Build a mock ecom store
- ❖ We have this issue with a client, how would you solve it, please include a presentation.
- ❖ Here is a list of functions, write them.

ETC...

Other companies will use a site like Hackerrank to send you a test on Algorithms and Data Structures, which are usually timed.

Then of course, you have the live coding exercises.

Let's cover these one by one, understand the best way to tackle them, what to do if you fail them and how to still get a win even through a fail.

1. The company's own tech test.

These are usually better for juniors than tests from sites which focus more on DS&A (data structures and algorithms).

They are better for a few reasons, You will usually get a week to complete them, they will be a task as opposed to a test, you can ask for help.

You will get an email which will consist of the contents of the task.

Sometimes, what the task is asking you to do can be a little confusing. A lot of people will feel put off from asking or clarifying what needs to be done, I highly recommend you ask.

Poke questions and make sure you 100% understand what the task is asking from you.

Your recruiter is there to see you succeed, not fail.

They will be more than happy to clarify any queries and even offer some advice.

The worst thing you can do is to try to attempt a task you do not understand, you will end up down a rabbit hole of Stack Overflow and Doritos.

As with any problem break down the test into tasks, if you need to create a mock website, for example;

1. Research websites
2. Decide on tech
3. Create header
4. Create body
5. Create footer
6. Add menu
7. Connect menu pages
8. Add social media handles

And so on and so forth.

Broken down, the test becomes less scary and more manageable.

You can use Trello to create a board and share this as a part of your interview.

Being able to work with task management boards is a huge advantage, Creating and using tickets, etc.

If you get stuck, like with making a header or menu, for example, then always Google first.

Try and find answers, as more than likely the question you have has been asked before.

If you still struggle, then fall back on friends and your network. Ask for some guidance from a senior or someone more experienced you know.

The important thing here is that they DO NOT write the code for you, but prompt you to an answer which may be more suited or offer some advice of how they may have approached the task.

This way you are learning as you would on the job, benefitting from the input of someone with more experience but also learning a new approach and thinking about a better solution.

I will go more into building a network and personal brand on social media in later chapters.

So, we have covered some bits on attempting tech tests from companies who have their own test.

However, what if you fail the test or do not have the time to complete it? I mean you probably have a full time job, a family, life and responsibilities.

Well, you can still land the job...

Another example, from the fantastic life of Zack...

The interview for my second role involved a tech test. It was a bit of a challenge, writing an algorithm to take a bunch of letters and find the words in a huge list from a JSON file which these letters can spell.

During this time I had life to contend with, kids and Coronavirus working its way through my house.

Long story short, I did not finish the test partly because of life, secondly I got stuck on writing the algorithm.

So, I decided what I would do is submit the work I did and write the steps of what I would do and how I would attempt the rest had I some more time.

A week later I got an interview. A week after that I got a job offer.

Moral of the story?

Finishing the test is great, but not finishing it does not rule you out from getting the job.

Even if you get stuck, write out what you would like to have done next, what you think would be a good solution and how that solution would be beneficial or scalable.

You maybe pleasantly surprised.

2. Hackerrank tests

FYI Hackerrank is not the only site companies use to send tests. It is just the one I received the most.

Hackerrank tests mainly focus on data structures & algorithms (DS&A). They are a timed test, usually two questions and you get around 90 minutes to complete.

Once you complete the algorithms you can run a test against your answer then submit it.

This is shit scary.

Well, it is when you start out. Most self-taught programmers start off with web dev and know very little about DS&A, same with bootcamp grads.

Attempting a test like that can be very difficult for a couple of reasons.

Timed tests add pressure, attempting a question on DS&A as a junior web dev can totally throw you, you will have less time to find help, unless you come from an academic background understanding the question itself can be very difficult.

On top of that, you rarely will have an opportunity to submit any work after the deadline to support your test, although you can submit half finished tests online.

The best thing to do is just try. When attempting a test like this, I prefer to use my desktop IDE, e.g. Visual Studio Code or IntelliJ, Android Studio etc.

It is more comfortable for me and I find I can work much more efficiently.

I copy the question down and begin to work on a solution.

Once complete, copy and paste it back to the online editor making sure it works on there.

A couple of tips, again, Google is your friend. You will likely be able to find previous solutions from other people.

IF you decide to use somebody else's code, please, at least understand it. Break it down, know what each part of it is doing then make some changes.

If you get asked about your solution and know nothing about it, your interview will quickly fall apart.

However, writing your own solution is much more beneficial.

It is a good idea to practice beforehand.

Before you attempt a test, or if you have some spare time, once a week spend an hour or two attempting the practice questions on the Hackerrank website.

It is a fantastic way to get more comfortable answering DS&A questions, you will also probably end up practicing a question you may even get asked.

3. Live coding exercises

The ultimate pressure on a junior developer.

As if asking you to spend all your time developing a full stack application with a presentation wasn't enough, they now also want you to live code.

Great.

'Breathe...1...2...3'

Live coding interviews are my least favourite type of test.

They add un-needed pressure and having three people stare at you whilst saying 'Do not worry, just act like we are not here' does not help whatsoever.

You are there, I can hear you breathing down your microphone, Stephen.

Depending on the company these can vary. They are usually a 20 minute - 1 hour exercise which maybe something like;

- ❖ Reverse an array of ints and add them all together
- ❖ Create a method which takes an argument and returns so and so
- ❖ Something like the world renowned FizzBuzz exercise.

If you get Fizzbuzz consider yourself lucky, more than likely, you have done it before.

Even the most simple tasks become a lot harder in a live coding interview.

However, here are some things to remember which may take the pressure off a little.

The people conducting the interview love questions, well most of them. Ask them about a preferred language, or to clarify any part of the task.

Using Google is ok.

What you may not realise is that the live coding exercise is more so about how you would solve the problem than if you actually do.

In 20 - 40 minutes most interviewers will not be expecting you to solve it.

What they do like to see is how you use Stack Overflow or Google and other resources to find a solution, how do you think about a problem and lastly your coding ability, it is a junior position after all.

I also recommend using this opportunity to talk to the interviewers about life at the company.

Now, here is a little snippet from our sponsor, the life of Zack...

My first live coding interview I absolutely failed. I do not mean it went bad, I mean it went horrific.

All I had to do was take an array of numbers as a string, convert them to integers then add them together.

There were three people watching me, I was in my bedroom in my best shirt with sweat patches galore.

Sounds simple right? I mean, I could do it with my eyes closed. I totally panicked under pressure and my mind went blank.

In the last ten minutes I really needed to wee. So, I asked to be excused, when I came back they pretty much all told me they needed to go and that was enough for them.

Needless to say I made a total shit show of it.

Not only did I not complete the task, I also felt totally embarrassed that people were watching me.

I had a second live coding interview, with another company a week later, where they asked me to fetch data from an API.

I nailed it, considering it was a much more difficult task, doesn't really make sense does it?

However, I was more comfortable than in my first.

Live coding tests can be cruel.

Try and do your best to block out the idea that people are there.

You are just in your comfort zone writing some code.

Use Google, Stack Overflow and make some mistakes, find some answers.

If it does not go well, try not to let it beat you down.

Just remember, it is not just you it is happening too. I felt like a total idiot, but learned a lesson.

Pressure creates diamonds.

TAKE AWAY

Tech tests and coding interviews are horrible. Very generic and can be very embarrassing.

Try your best. You can do no more than your best.

If you fail to complete it, follow it up anyway with an email on what you would have liked to have done.

They are not designed to catch you out, a lot of them are not even designed to be finished.

How you approach the task, handle it and attempt to find solutions are just as important.

Don't get flustered. On the job you will have many moments of having to think and find answers under-pressure.

In pair-programming exercises, talk out loud about what you are doing and why you are doing it. It helps you to think about what you are doing and the person watching to understand why.

7. Show me the money.

> If you are going through a career change, the salary on offer may seem a little low to what you may have been on previously. A small cut may be necessary to land a first junior role, however, do feel confident to ask for a higher amount. Explain about your living situation, if they like you, they will be happy to accommodate where they can.

So far, we have talked about steps to take to land your first, or even second role as a junior software engineer.

Fantastic news, you have been made an offer, but what does it mean? What questions should you ask at offer stage?

This is a really exciting time, I mean, all the hard work you put in… coding in your spare time, working, building projects, using Git, applying to everything has paid off!

You should just dive straight in and accept, right?

Heck no.

You need to take a moment, pace yourself.

Think.

Congratulations on getting your offer. I am really happy for you, I also want to make sure you are getting the best deal you can.

At the end of the day, you will only become as good as the people you work with and the company you work for.

Is there a training budget for you?

Are you going to get exposure to different tech?

Will there be the opportunity to grow and take on more responsibilities?

What hardware do they use?

Do you need to be in the office everyday or can you work from home?

Do you need flexible working hours?

These are all extremely valid and solid questions you should feel totally comfortable to ask.

Often, when I speak to people who have been offered a role or who are at final interview stage they are apprehensive or worried to ask direct questions.

Don't be.

I wasn't and I am still not.

I need to know that the company I am working will give me training opportunities. That they will allow me movement to grow and become a senior engineer.

Think about where you want to be in a few years, senior engineer? Tech lead? Maybe in a different team, DevOps engineer?

I don't always want to be in the office, so working from home two days a week is a big plus.

How about you? Will working from home two days a week allow you to save time and costs on commuting?

Flexible working hours helps me with my kids.

You may not have children, but you may have other caring commitments.

There are also vital questions about the company culture, If the job adverts say free beer and pizza on a Friday, I am instantly put off.

Don't get me wrong. It is totally cool at a meet-up, to me though, it just screams bro culture or 'we want to be a cool tech place too.'

Somehow pizza and beer is now the epitome of cool we have landed at.

One of my favourite things to do and one I highly recommend is to approach current and former employees on LinkedIn.

I know, a little bit stalker-ish!

However, it works. More often than not current and former employees are more than willing to share their experiences of the company and the culture.

Who better to tell you about life at the company than the people working there, not the people trying to get you to work there.

If you go down this route, it is worth first asking your recruiter if they could recommend anyone from the company who would be willing to speak to you.

Lastly, the salary itself.

If, like me, you are a career changer then you will likely end up taking a pay cut to some degree.

Coming into a new industry as a fresh faced junior, they cannot exactly be throwing the stacks of cash at you…yet, anyway.

According to Glassdoor, the average junior developer salary is £26,106 per year. I will add, I go through a lot of junior developer job specs and I would say for a graduate it is accurate.

Apprenticeships or Bootcamp grads may often get offered a little less, due to the lack of foundational knowledge you would gain from three years in academia.

Just to give you some insight, almost all Bootcamp grads I have worked with were offered roles in the region of £18 - £22k

You have a life to live and bills to pay. If you find yourself with an offer which is at the lower end of the scale, but it isn't enough for you to get by on, then let them know.

A friend of mine did with his first offer and instantly got a 2k pay bump.

Success!

All it takes is a little bravery.

You cannot work a job that you cannot afford to be at.

TAKE AWAY

Congratulations, you got a job offer!

Think before committing, Use every opportunity you have had up until now to ask every question you can ask.

Ask the uncomfortable questions - salary, growth, flexibility etc.

Talk to previous and current employees about their experiences and thoughts on the company.

All of this will allow you to understand the company better and overall you will feel more comfortable that you will be bringing value to the company and more importantly to yourself.

I and many others are firm believers that you will only become as good as the people you work with.

If the firm has a great deal of experienced developers you will have a good pool of people to learn from.

8. Social media...ah shit.

> Keep your LinkedIn up to date! I personally have found LinkedIn to be a fantastic tool for leveraging and attracting recruiters, so long as you use it to its potential. Do you want to be a junior developer? Then add junior developer to your title. If you are learning to code, you are a junior developer.
>
> Write posts about what you have been working on, share content from other parts of the web. It does not have to be technical and you do not need to know all the answers, but what you share will carry on around as your network grows.

Social media…Ah shit!

Yes, It has been said to me before.

Social media, we all know it and often we have a love/hate relationship with it.

We love to like, share, comment.

We hate to make, write or design content.

Browsing LinkedIn, Insta, TikTok is way fun, however, in your position, they can become powerful tools for landing jobs.

Not only can you have recruiters hounding you, you can also have companies reaching out to you directly.

The best networks for the technology industry are Twitter and LinkedIn.

LinkedIn for me has been invaluable, I am constantly messaged by recruiters, my network grows and grows plus I have gotten opportunities and networked with people whom I would never have had the chance to without it.

How can you use LinkedIn effectively as a junior or aspiring developer?

Let's go through it. I am going to share a sort of blueprint I have been working on.

This isn't a teaser for a course you need to buy, this is free, solid information for you.

LinkedIn is a platform dedicated to the working and professional world, people scroll it for fun and more just as much as Facebook and Insta.

The way to get seen is by creating, writing and sharing content, finally having a complete profile will allow you to appear in more recruiters searches.

The more you do the wider your network will expand and the more eyes will land upon you and your aim for a job.

Sounds like a lot of work, right?

Well, maybe not so.

You do not need to be a seasoned pro to share content.

1. Post regularly
2. What to post
3. Like and comment

1. Post regularly

One of the best ways to expand your circle is to write unique content. As with any social media site unique content is always rewarded with a wider reach.

Now, this can quickly become laborious.

Sticking to a posting schedule can help keep this regular and take off some of the pressure.

I set an alarm for 9.30am everyday, at that point I try to post something, whether it be a thought, idea, feeling etc.

It does not mean I post everyday, somedays I am caught in an extended stand up or I am struggling with a 4 and 6 year old while trying to write some code or debug something I've made a mess of.

The reminder is there, though. It is unto you how you respond to it.

2. What to post?

The best posts are engaging, maybe pose a question, or ask for an opinion or ideas. As your network grows more and more people are likely to respond.

In my early days I would take screen shots or videos of an app or program I was writing, and share a little something about it.

It could be something you've learned about the language or something you think could be beneficial to other people in your network.

The point being, you do not need to be an expert to share. People will relate to your level and you may even get some advice or applause.

If you do not want to share your project, maybe just something that has come across your mind about the industry.

Sometimes I post random thoughts. Go back through my post history, you will know what I mean.

Subscribing to tech news blogs and following hashtags which are related to your industry allows you to re-share trending content.

Add your thoughts to it and ask for opinions. Great way to keep yourself up-to date and engage in conversation with your network.

3. Get those likes flowing!

Liking and re-sharing content from people you follow and more active developers can help increase your engagement.

Start engaging through comments with people, ask questions about a piece of work, give a congratulations or even start a debate!

People love responding to comments, it gets you noticed by everybody else who looks at the post and it shows your interest in the industry.

I make it a point, at least a few times a day to congratulate or support somebody in the industry with either a few words of positive reinforcement or a congratulations for landing a role.

Again, it keeps your account active, healthy and you are well on your way to becoming a small influencer in the developer community.

Your network is growing, you're becoming known as a positive, great person with a real community attitude.

Pretty soon them job offers are going to start rolling in!

The last thing I will cover is your profile.

LinkedIn will reward you for having a fully optimised profile, that reward is in the form of appearing in more recruiter searches.

In-fact, LinkedIn says All-Star profiles are 40x more likely to receive job opportunities!

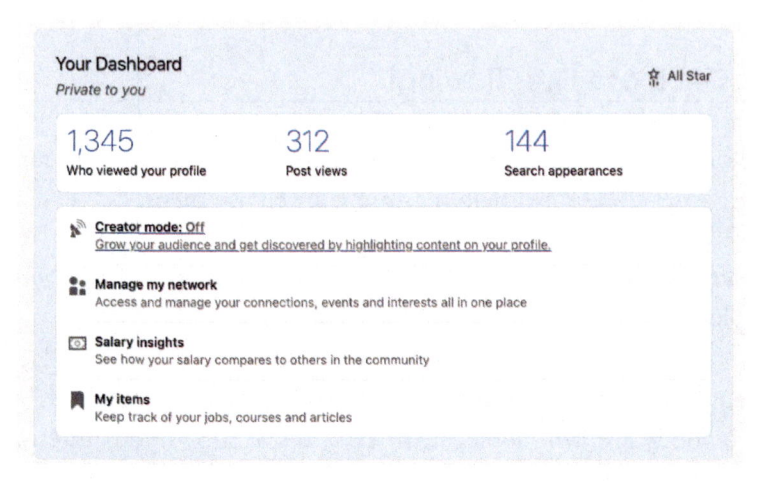

In the top right section of the image above you can see the 'All Star', which means I have completed all the steps necessary to have the strongest profile.

The eight steps to an 'All Star' profile are;

1. **A great profile image**

A relatively simple yet effective thing to have. Take an image with a clear background whether that is colourful or black / white is up to you.

2. A stand out Headline

This is where you will catch the attention of the search engine and recruiters. I suggest 'junior software engineer' over 'aspiring' etc. This will allow you to appear via search terms which are actually being used.

3. Industry & Location

Make sure to add your country and industry, an easy thing to do.

4. Experience

Add in all your previous roles and current, whether related or not. A lot of people have wonderful transferable skills from other industries without even knowing.

5. Skills

Add your skills and do not be shy! A minimum of five with as many more as you can think of. Sell yourself.

6. Summary

Your summary can be difficult to write. I suggest keeping it brief with a description about you, your achievements and goals.

7. Education

Adding your places of education allows your network to grow as you can connect with people who attended the same institutes.

8. Connections

Add people whom you think you can learn from or add value too. When adding new people, it is courteous to add a little message introducing yourself and why you want to connect.

TAKE AWAY

Let the jobs come to you!

Start off with a small reminder to post a couple of times a week. You can also use content scheduling software, like buffer, to pre-write and set content.

You do not have to write the most amazing content in the world, share an update to a project, a screen shot or re-share some tech news with your thoughts about it.

Comment on other peoples posts and pretty soon your network will start to grow.

Get that profile optimised! Having a fully optimised profile will allow you to stand out massively in job searches and give you that 'All Star' status, which according to LinkedIn gives you a tremendous boost in the search results which means more recruiters eyes are on you!

9. We have anxiety too!

> **Attending meet-ups and hackathons are a great way to network and even get a job.**
>
> **Tech people are usually very friendly and welcoming to fresh faces. Go say hello, even if you struggle with social situations you will find many of us have the same fears.**

For the most part, tech people are some of the geekiest and most welcoming people you can meet.

The thought of attending a meet-up or networking event will instantly give most of us insane sweat patches and butterfly stomachs.

However, what you will find, attending that meet-up will probably be one of the best moves of your career.

Meet-ups are heavily underrated in terms of how hooked up you can become to the tech world in your local community.

Meet-ups are usually hosted by people who are incredibly passionate about growing a community, they are often hard work with little or no financial reward.
Speaking as someone who worked in the tech events industry for a while.

We spoke in the previous chapter about using social media sites like LinkedIn to grow your online network and slowly let the recruiters do the job for you.

The same can be done with tech meet-ups and networking events.

Recruiters often attend them and what you will find is once you settle in and make some friends they will also be more than happy to recommend you for roles that become available at the companies they work for(or even own).

Meet-ups offer so much variety in terms of what you can do and learn. Many focus on a single technology or a group of technologies, which you can become an expert in from attending.

As much focus as I put on building an online network and applying for every job, you should also put into attending and interacting at meet-ups and tech events.

If you are someone who struggles socially, or detest the thought of social interaction, hey, you're not alone!

Many of us also have a form of social anxiety.

We are not going to judge you for it, heck come and join in with our socially awkward talk.

Pretty soon, you will feel more comfortable and even make friends for life.

You will realise this is a community of support and we want you to become a part of it.

There are meet-ups all around and for all sorts of purposes and technologies.
Groups for women, groups based on sexual preference, gender and more.

I run the Manchester Google Developer Group and there are fantastic GDG's all around the UK and the world.

Have a look around, you may be surprised how long you may have been living somewhere with a fantastic tech community waiting for you to join.

TAKE AWAY

Networking IRL is just as important as networking online. Hit them meet-ups!

A lot of time recruiters or people who are aware of roles available in companies are there.

If you struggle socially, try not to worry. A lot of us do too.

We are not there to judge, we want you to feel supported, engaged and join our community.

Many people find jobs through recommendations from attending meet-ups and hackathons. You will also meet new friends from all walks of life.

Lastly, it is a fantastic way to learn new things and you may find you come out an expert before you even land your first role.

BREAK TIME

At this point. We have covered some major points. Primarily all of which are to do with landing your first role.

We've talked about

- ❖ GitHub and demonstrating your learning journey.
- ❖ Projects to make you stand out.
- ❖ Applying for roles
- ❖ Tech tests
- ❖ Negotiating an offer
- ❖ Using LinkedIn and meet ups to land a role.

Going forward we will briefly cover life after you land a job, whether that is your first or second role in the industry.

How mindset and imposter syndrome can take you by surprise.

What to expect and how to keep improving.

10. Code makes us all cry.

> *You will feel over-whelmed in your first and second role. Do not worry! It is perfectly normal and happens to everyone. Take a deep breath and just know this is an industry where you can go from working on something very simple to something very intense, take it in your stride and try your best.*

This job isn't about knowing it all.

I mean, if you do, congratulations.

For the other 99% of us though, the important thing is knowing how to solve problems, how to try and most importantly, how to ask for help.

You may be someone who has built a few passion projects, followed some tutorials or even attended a bootcamp.

Now, though, you're in the big leagues.

You landed your first role.

You get assigned your first ticket.

Cry?

Ok, just this once, but then it's time to put on your software engineer hat.

Cause you got this!

Large code bases can be over-whelming, especially when starting out, even attempting tasks in a professional environment can add pressure.

Do not stress!

Remember, you are a junior.

1. Try your best
2. There is nothing you can do to ruin it
3. Know when to ask for help
4. When things get really tough

1. Try your best

If you have moments of thinking 'oh, shit what have I done, is this industry for me? Can I do this? Have I made a mistake?'

Trust me when I scream this, YOU ARE NOT ALONE!!!!

Imposter syndrome hits everyone at some point.

It can be frustrating, annoying, make you doubt every fibre in your being.

However, **you are amazing**.

You have worked so hard to get where you are, you studied when everyone else slept, you set your goals and never stopped, you had the drive, the determination and fortitude to never give up.

You deserve to be sat there, working for that company and you will be able to write that code.

When you get a ticket, task or asked to do something, just try.

One of the best things you can do is to just try. Quite often, as human beings we are afraid of being outside of our comfort zone. However, never underestimate the power of just trying. You may even surprise yourself before surprising those around you.

Understand the problem, ask questions about the project to have a greater understanding of how it works and what the end goal is.

Google solutions if you get stuck, write the code and try it.

Doesn't work?

Re-write it and try it again.

Give it your damn best.

You **cannot** do anymore than your best.

Always try before asking for help, but always ask for help to understand the problem before trying.

2. There is nothing you can do to ruin it

This is something you should definitely take a moment to understand.

You will not have privileges to push or make changes to a master branch of a repo.

Think of the master branch as the final destination of all of your and the other developers code. Where it all comes together to form a whole piece of software.

When you start a new ticket, to implement new or update some existing code you will 'branch off' the master.

Any work you do will be on your branch and it will not affect the master branch.

Any work you do will be checked over by a minimum of one senior engineer before being merged into the master branch.

You cannot break the software. All checks are done before merging your code back into the master branch.

In the unfortunate event that merging a branch into the master causes some unusual or bad behaviour, it can be debugged or the code can restored to the previous version before the branch was merged in.

Do not fear breaking things. Often, things will get broke before getting fixed.

Your title as a junior allows you the affordability to break things, without repercussions.

Breaking things means fixing things.

Ultimately, this leads to lessons learned.

3. Know when to ask for help

Knowing when and how to ask for help is one of your greatest weapons as a junior dev.

This leads on from point number 1, always try first.

If you try and do not succeed…it is ok! In fact it is more than OK, as the chances are you are now about to learn something.

However, there is an appropriate way to ask for help, and often it isn't 'I cannot do this, help me'

Rather, a better way to ask for help would be.

'I was assigned this task, I thought *this* would be the best way to solve it, I tried *this* which didn't work, so I found *this* solution on Stack Overflow, Now I am a little stuck, could you help?'

People are willing to help people who are willing to help themselves.

When you try a few things, you are showing your enthusiasm to learn, you did some research on the task and may even have found a better way to do it, you just lack the experience to implement it.

This is amazing.

Now, instead of having someone else solve the problem, ask if you can pair program on it.

Even better, you're now getting some exposure to another developers way of thinking and you're writing some pretty cool code!

One of the worst things you can do is to sit and struggle.

If you cannot do the task, do not sit there thinking how hard it is, how much of a failure you are for hours or even days.

If you have tried your best, have Googled and Stack Overflowed your brains out, it's time to ask for help.

The longer you leave it, the more behind you will fall which can have an impact on deadlines and your team.

A tech lead may even give you a tough ticket or task to do as a test to see whether you will sit and struggle or ask for help!

4. When things get really tough.

I realise on the days when it feels like you have no idea why you even decided to travel down this route, it can be tough.

Mentally, learning and writing code is difficult as it is. Never mind with the added pressure from life and those around us.

It is at moments like these when I step away from the screen and have a little 'me' time. Or 'dumb days' as I have come to call them.

It is a day, or a few hours, where I do something I want to do. It isn't productive, nor often even creative. A couple of weeks ago I played Red Dead Redemption 1, for 12 hours straight on my Xbox. I ate chicken wings and I did nothing else.

On the weekends, I try to hike. This clears my mind and reconnects me with new thoughts and ideas.

For you, it maybe something else. May be you go to the gym, or for a run. You could throw axes or read a book.

You need to find your vice which helps you disconnect from the code and reconnect with your body and mind, especially at this early stage in your career. The later you will appreciate that you took the time to learn to switch off.

TAKE AWAY

Being a software engineer is tough!

There is nothing you can do to break or damage the code you are writing. There are measures in place to have your code reviewed and checked before being approved.

Early in your career you will be tested and it can be very overwhelming. Just know that many people struggle with imposter syndrome.

You have worked exceptionally hard to get where you are, you should be proud. Improvement comes in small steps which add up over time.

Always try first, then ask for help. More often than not you will be able to find full or partial answers to your questions.

When you feel like you have done all that you can do, then it is time to reach out. Never struggle for longer than you need.

Ask for help with the aim of presenting what you have tried first, it will show that you have a 'problem solvers' mindset and you are not just unwilling to try.

Finally, once you get the help - learn from it. Ask questions to whomever it is taking the time to teach you something. It may also be a great opportunity to pair program.

11. Failure happens, success is imminent.

> *Failure is a part of success. From junior to senior failure happens. What matters more is the willingness to learn from it, dust yourself off and keep going forward.*

Everybody fails at something. Whether that be a test, a sport..anything.

I will hold my hands up, I failed at a few things. My driving test first time round, my GCSE's, education and much more.

When it came to my career change, I felt like more of a failure than I had ever done in my life.

It was not just me I was doing It for, it was my wife, my kids and our future. No matter how dumb I felt, I knew I had to keep going.

What allowed me to get to where I am now, though, is my persistence in the face of a challenge, my determination to be better, my boundless enthusiasm to never be put down.

At the point of writing this book;
- I taught myself to code.
- I changed my career at the age of 29, with two kids and a family to provide for.
- I succeeded as a mobile developer.
- I got my second role as a full stack developer.
- I got accepted as a Google Developer Group lead.
- I started juniordeveloper.careers to help other juniors.
- I landed my 3rd role as a software data engineer for one of the UKs biggest health companies.

The list goes on.

This book, though, this story, isn't about me.

It's about you.

This is the start of your journey.

The start of your career.

It is your story.

When you feel like life is becoming a little overwhelming, take a moment for yourself. Plan a couple of hours a week for you to do you.

When the job takes its toll on you, have a day away from the screen.

One day a week, read a book. A real book, not a kindle book.

You have done amazing. You will continue to do amazing.

I sincerely hope this book gave you the understanding, the energy and the boost you need to continue your job search.

I pray you land your job in the tech industry.

I know you're going to kick butt!

If you found this book helpful, let me know.

Maybe you can think of another subject which may help others which you feel should be covered in here?

Let me know.

For now, though.

Get out there and let the world know you're not taking any prisoners.

What I need from you

Thank you for reading through my book. As many of you know I dedicate a lot of my (limited) free time to helping people such as yourselves land their first and second jobs in this industry. To do that, though takes a lot of work and as such I am going to ask 5 things off of you:

1. Go to my website juniordeveloper.careers and upload your CV, the more CVs I have the more companies I can get to post jobs on there.

2. Follow me on [Linkedin](#) - Ishaq Amin

3. Follow me on [Twitter](#) - digitalGuyZack

4. Follow my LinkedIn page [JuniorDeveloper.careers](#)

5. Share your thoughts on this book on your socials and tag me!

The more you can help me with the above, the more resources I can build for everyone of us.

Common interview questions / tech test skills for junior positions

A brief overview of common questions I, and others, have been asked in an interview which you should definitely be able to answer and some skills which will come in handy.

This isn't expansive but they cover a wide variety of skills and questions which will improve your overall understand and skills.

Javascript

Tasks
1. Find the highest number in an array
2. Find the lowest number in an array
3. Sort the numbers in an array
4. Remove duplicates from an array
5. Find an item in an array
6. Reverse the words in a string

Questions
1. How does scope work in Javascript?
2. When do we use const and let?
3. What is the difference between let and var?
4. What is the difference between == and ===?
5. What is the difference between asynchronous and synchronous.
6. What is a promise?

React

Tasks
1. Call data from this API
2. Create a website which shows these pictures
3. Have a submit button which saves the input or sends it to a backend.

Questions
1. What is state?
2. Tell me about Redux?
3. Explain a hook you've used recently and why?
4. How does a callback work?
5. Tell me about data binding?

Node

Tasks
1. Create an endpoint
2. Create a function which goes over a JSON file and returns an item
3. Create an endpoint which returns an array of data when hit

Questions
1. What is express?
2. Tell me about the FS module?
3. What does a 500 error represent?
4. How do you import a module in Node compared to React?

Python

Tasks
1. Iterate over an array
2. Generate a random number between 1 and 10

Questions
1. What is a lambda function?
2. Difference between a list and tuple?
3. Can you use OOP in python?
4. What are python modules? Example of one?
5. Does python use camel case naming convention?
6. What does the break keyword do?

Printed in Great Britain
by Amazon